Sugar Inspirations

Celebration Runouts

CARON MATHIAS

MEREHURST

Dedication

This book is dedicated to my loving husband Malcolm, for his support, encouragement and patience, and to my son Gareth, for all his help with his baby sister Kayleigh.

First published 1996 by Merehurst Limited
Ferry House, 51–57 Lacy Road, Putney,
London SW15 1PR

Copyright © Merehurst Limited 1996
ISBN 1-85391-569-6

A catalogue record for this book is available from the British Library.

Editor: Helen Southall
Design: Anita Ruddell
Photography by James Duncan

Colour separation by Bright Arts,
Hong Kong

Printed in Hong Kong
by Wing King Tong

Acknowledgements

The author would like to thank the following:

Kingsley Cards Ltd.
Catsbrain Farm
Worminghall Road
Oakley, Aylesbury
Bucks HP18 9UL

Fine Art Developments plc.
Dawson Lane, Dudley Hill
Bradford
West Yorkshire BD4 6HW

The publishers would like to thank the following suppliers:

Cake Art Ltd.
Venture Way
Crown Estate
Priorswood, Taunton
Devon TA2 8DE

Guy, Paul & Co. Ltd.
Unit B4
Foundry Way
Little End Road
Eaton Socon
Cambs PE19 3JH

Squires Kitchen
Squires House
3 Waverley Lane
Farnham
Surrey GU9 8BB

Anniversary House (Cake Decorations) Ltd.
Unit 5
Roundways
Elliott Road
Bournemouth BH11 8JJ

Contents

Introduction

Decorative and appealing, runout sugar pieces add character and charm to any celebration cake.

This book is designed to encourage and inspire sugarcraft enthusiasts to experiment with royal icing and produce new and exciting ideas for standing runouts. I have endeavoured to include various techniques, suitable for a variety of occasions, and, with a little practice and patience, anyone can achieve a high standard of work, whatever their level of experience.

Equipment for Runouts

The following is a list of basic equipment needed to make the standing runouts in this book. Many of the items are standard kitchen, craft or cake-making equipment; any other items required for individual projects are listed on the relevant pages.

- Greaseproof (waxed) paper piping bags and piping tubes (tips), see page 6
- Smooth flat boards for drying runouts
- Angle-poise lamp
- Masking tape
- Scissors
- Tracing paper and pencil
- Drawings and designs (see pages 43-48)

- Waxed paper or clear runout film
- Palette knife and scraper
- Small mixing bowl and teaspoon
- Damp cloth
- Foam pad and pieces
- Paintbrush
- Paste food colourings
- Absorbent kitchen paper

Basic Recipes

Royal Icing

Either pure or substitute albumen can be used in this icing, though pure albumen makes stronger standing runouts. For extra-strong pieces, use double-strength albumen, i.e. 2 tablespoons albumen powder to 4 tablespoons water.

1 tablespoon albumen powder (pure or substitute)
4 tablespoons water
500g (1lb/3 cups) icing (confectioners') sugar

1 Whisk the albumen powder and water together. If using pure albumen powder, leave to stand until dissolved.

2 Sift the icing sugar into the bowl of an electric mixer,

and strain in the albumen. Beat at the slowest speed for approximately 3 minutes to reach the soft peak stage; 4 minutes for full peak (explained in more detail on page 6).

3 Use the icing straight away or place in a container, cover with a damp cloth and seal with an airtight lid. Store in the refrigerator.

Royal Icing for Extension Work

Preparation of icing for extension work is very important. Use finer-grade sugar, i.e. bridal icing (confectioners') sugar, and sift it 2–3 times. I use fresh egg white instead of albumen powder in extension work icing, but it is a matter of preference. Add gum arabic for strength and liquid glucose for stretch.

300g (10oz/2 cups) bridal icing (confectioners') sugar
1 egg white (size 2)
¼ teaspoon gum arabic
½ teaspoon liquid glucose

1 Sift the icing sugar 2–3 times, finally sifting it into the bowl of an electric mixer. Strain the egg white into the bowl, and mix on the slowest speed for 2 minutes. Add the gum arabic and mix for 1 minute more. Finally, add the glucose and mix for a further 1 minute.

⟨2⟩ Store the icing in an airtight container. Before piping, pass the amount of icing required, a little at a time, through a fine piece of stocking or muslin. This is a very successful method of eliminating small particles, making it easier to use very fine piping tubes (tips).

Flower Paste

There are many different flower paste recipes so it is best to experiment to see which one works for you. This recipe contains more egg white and fat than traditional recipes, and therefore produces a paste with a longer working time than most. By using both gum tragacanth and gum tragacanth substitute (CMC), the paste is elastic to use but still sets hard.

2 teaspoons powdered gelatine
5 teaspoons cold water
500g (1lb/3 cups) icing (confectioners') sugar
2 teaspoons gum tragacanth
2 teaspoons gum tragacanth substitute (carboxymethylcellulose/CMC)
2 teaspoons liquid glucose
5 teaspoons white vegetable fat (shortening)
1½ egg whites (size 2)

⟨1⟩ Add the gelatine to the cold water in a heatproof bowl, and leave to stand for 20 minutes.

⟨2⟩ Sift the icing sugar into an ovenproof bowl. Sprinkle the gum tragacanth and gum tragacanth substitute over the surface, and warm in the oven on a low temperature for 20 minutes.

⟨3⟩ Warm the liquid glucose in a small bowl or teacup over a saucepan of hot water until it is runny. Dissolve the gelatine over hot water, then remove from the heat, and add the glucose and white vegetable fat. Return to a low heat and stir until everything is dissolved and blended.

⟨4⟩ Heat the beater from an electric mixer. Place the warmed dry ingredients in the bowl of the mixer, add the gelatine mixture and egg white, and mix on a slow speed until all the ingredients are combined. Turn the mixer to maximum speed, and beat for about 5 minutes or until the paste is white and stringy. Transfer the paste to a clean plastic bag and store in an airtight container in the refrigerator for 24 hours before using.

Pastillage (Quick Method)

This pastillage is quick and easy to produce and is ideal for making small cut-out pieces and plaques. Make sure the gum tragacanth is the best quality, i.e. pure white in appearance.

½ teaspoon gum tragacanth
3 tablespoons royal icing (full peak, see page 6)
1 tablespoon cornflour (cornstarch)

⟨1⟩ Stir the gum tragacanth into the royal icing, cover with a damp cloth, and leave to stand for 1 hour before using.

⟨2⟩ Turn the paste on to a board and work in the cornflour until the paste has the consistency of sugarpaste. Double-wrap the paste in two plastic bags to prevent drying out. Store in a sealed container in the refrigerator or in a cool place.

Modelling Paste

This paste is suitable for making frills and modelling.

60g (2oz) flower paste
60g (2oz) sugarpaste
white vegetable fat (shortening)

⟨1⟩ Mix the two pastes thoroughly together. If the mixture becomes sticky, blend in a little white vegetable fat.

⟨2⟩ Use the paste straight away or store in a plastic bag in an airtight container.

Edible glues

Either of the following recipes can be used as an alternative to egg white for attaching paste to runouts.

Gum Glue

1 tablespoon boiled water or rose water
1 teaspoon gum arabic

⟨1⟩ Sterilize equipment with boiling water, and leave to dry.

5

2 Put the boiled water or rose water in a heatproof bowl or teacup, and sprinkle the gum arabic on to the surface. Heat over a saucepan of hot water until dissolved. Strain into a sterilized container.

Sugarpaste Glue

30g (1oz) sugarpaste
1 tablespoon water

Put the sugarpaste and water in a small heatproof bowl or teacup and heat over a saucepan of hot water until dissolved, stirring occasionally.

Runout Techniques

Making piping bags

The piping tubes (tips) used and referred to throughout this book are Bekenal piping tubes. To make paper piping bags that fit the tubes, cut a 38 x 25cm (15 x 10 inch) sheet of greaseproof (waxed) paper to make small, medium or large bags (see diagrams below). Fold each piece into a cone shape.

Large

Medium

Small

Other types of paper, e.g. silicone paper or parchment, can be used to make piping bags, if preferred. Ready-made bags are also available from local suppliers.

Preparing royal icing

Royal icing required for runouts, coating and fine piping should be beaten in an electric mixer for 3 minutes to the 'soft peak' stage. To test the icing, dip the tip of a spoon into it and immediately lift the spoon out. The peak of icing that forms should fall to one side. (Allow 20 minutes if beating by hand.)

For piped shells and borders, the icing should be beaten for 4 minutes, to the 'full peak' stage. When carrying out the same test, the peak of icing should stand up. (Allow 25 minutes if beating by hand.)

Making runouts

When making runouts, it is important to use freshly beaten royal icing. To achieve 'runout' consistency, put 3 teaspoons of soft peak royal icing (see page 4, and above) on to a plastic scraper and, with a small palette knife, mix in a few droplets of water until the icing resembles thick cream (albumen may be added instead of water). Gently paddle the air bubbles out with the palette knife. To test for the correct consistency, carefully shake the scraper; the icing should just find its own level. For a larger quantity, put 3 tablespoons of royal icing in a bowl, and slowly stir in the water with a spoon. Mark a

figure-of-eight in the icing with the spoon; it should level out by the count of ten. Leave the icing to stand for 15 minutes.

Only half-fill the piping bag with runout icing; use a large bag for collars, etc., and a small or medium bag for filling in sections of a picture, depending on the size.

If using colour, blend it in well before thinning the icing. (Do not use glycerine for runout work as it would inhibit the drying process.)

1 Place your chosen design on a smooth, flat board, and cover with waxed paper. Smooth out the paper and secure at the corners with masking tape (which is easier to remove than sellotape).

2 Put some soft peak white royal icing into a grease-proof paper piping bag fitted with a no. 0 or no. 1 piping tube (tip) and pipe the outline of the design on to the waxed paper. (Coloured outlines can be piped if desired.)

3 Half-fill another bag with runout consistency royal icing. No tube is required for filling in (flooding) the runout. Cut off the end of the bag to the size of a no. 1 tube (tip) for small sections, and a no. 2 tube for larger sections. Start filling in the runout, first working on the areas that appear furthest away from you.

4 Gradually build up the picture using the various colours required. Leave each section for a few minutes to allow the icing to skin over before starting on the next. This will help define the different sections. If using very dark colours, like red or black, it is best to leave them to dry for slightly longer, especially if paler colours are to be piped next to them.

5 Use a paintbrush or the tip of the piping bag to help the icing into the corners, and break any air bubbles that appear on the surface. Raised areas, such as arms or clothing, can be created by piping two layers of icing. If pieces are to be added, like the scarf or lantern on the snowman, it is best to make the items separately and to add them when the runout is dry. Beginners might find it easier to number the picture with the best flooding order, as I have done for the snowman (see page 43).

6 When the runout is complete, immediately put it aside to dry under a form of direct heat for 1 hour. An angle-poise lamp, fitted with a 60-watt bulb or spotlight bulb and positioned 15–20cm (6–8 inches) away, is ideal. This will ensure a good sheen on the finished runout. After 1 hour, place the runout in a warm dry room for the remainder of the time. Smaller pieces need about 24 hours to dry thoroughly; larger runouts, such as collars, need 48 hours.

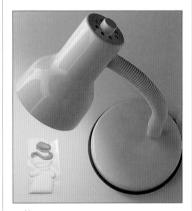

7 When thoroughly dry, remove the piece from the waxed paper. To do this, carefully peel off the masking tape, holding the picture in position, and gently pull the runout to the edge of the board. Carefully peel the paper off the back, releasing one part at a time. Turn the runout until it is free from the paper. Alternatively, slide a cranked palette knife under the runout to free it from the paper.

8 To flood the back of the runout, turn it over (it is not necessary to outline again), and fill in the various parts with runout consistency royal icing. Make sure the back view looks correct, i.e. the **back** of a head or body. To finish off, outline and highlight areas of the runout by hand-painting and adding any extra pieces. It is surprising how the finishing touches bring the subject to life.

Runout faults

* **Colour run**: runout icing too thin; insufficient drying time between sections.

* **Sinking**: drying process too long; damp conditions; runout icing too thin.

* **Not drying**: weak albumen; cold atmosphere for drying; old or insufficiently beaten icing.

* **Lack of shine**: runouts not dried under heat source e.g. angle-poise lamp.

* **Weak runouts**: weak albumen; too much colour added (some colours contain glycerine).

* **Wrinkled effect**: waxed paper melted under the heat; paper not flat on the board.

* **Cracked surface**: runout or waxed paper disturbed while icing is still wet.

* **Patchy runouts**: water not mixed in properly; colour not blended thoroughly.

* **Air bubbles**: water beaten into icing (*stir* in water and leave to stand for 15 minutes); icing bag used with large hole.

Frilling

Modelling paste can be used for most frilled pieces, but use flower paste for finer work. Sprinkle some cornflour (cornstarch) on to a non-stick board, and roll out the paste until it is thin. Cut out the required shapes, then, with a blunt-ended cocktail stick (toothpick), gently roll over the edge until the paste starts to lift from the board, creating a frilly effect. This can take some practice to perfect.

Colouring

The following food colourings are used throughout this book:

Droplet (liquid) colouring
Wedgewood blue

Paste colourings
Christmas red, liquorice black, cream, blueberry, chestnut, claret, melon, tangerine, dark brown, ice blue, mint green, mulberry, navy, paprika, egg yellow, autumn leaf, violet, Christmas green. For pale shades, use only a touch of colour, and for darker colours use about ¼ teaspoon, though the amount required will vary

depending on how much icing you are colouring. You can achieve some very good shades by blending two or three colours together. Mixing with white will tone colours down.

Powder colours (petal dusts/blossom tints)

Gold, peach, bluebell, moss green, pink, silver, white, brown, cream, skintone, autumn gold. When dusting with powder colours, take care not to use too much. Tone strong colours down with cornflour (cornstarch) or white petal dust, and use a large flat or rounded paintbrush.

Hand-painting

Completed runouts are mainly painted freehand, although detail such as faces can be marked out lightly with a pencil. To transfer a picture on to a cake or plaque, lightly scribe the design with a sharp instrument. Alternatively, the design can be 'traced' on to the surface of a cake or runout. To do this, first trace the design from the original on to tracing paper, then turn the paper over and go over the design with a soft pencil. Turn the paper over again and position it on the runout or cake. Go over the design again with a pencil so that the pencil on the back of the paper is transferred to the surface beneath.

Use good quality paintbrushes in varying sizes, e.g. nos. 00, 0, 1 and 2, and paste or powder food colourings. Mix the colour in a palette with some clear alcohol (gin or vodka),

until it has a smooth consistency. Use a piece of absorbent kitchen paper to dab any excess moisture off the brush, as this would melt the surface of the icing.

Study the picture carefully and mix the colours in various shades to achieve the best effect. Paint in the background first, then gradually build up the picture, adding detail and highlighting, and outlining prominent areas if necessary. If a longer period of time is required for painting, mix the colours with water as this does not evaporate as quickly as alcohol. Gold and silver, however, must be mixed with alcohol.

Using pastillage

Use the recipe for quick-method pastillage on page 5. Roll the paste out on a work surface sprinkled with a little cornflour (cornstarch) until it is thin. Icing (confectioners') sugar can be used for rolling out pastillage but it is easily absorbed into the paste and, as a result, the paste could stick. Keep the paste on the move, turning it round as you roll, and turn it over to smooth both sides before cutting out the shapes. It is necessary to work very quickly with pastillage as it begins to dry as soon as it is exposed to the atmosphere. Have all the templates ready, and cut out straight away. Leave to dry on a smooth, flat board, turning the pieces at 15-minute intervals for the first hour to help them dry flat and even. Small pieces will need about 2 hours in all to dry completely; larger pieces should be left overnight. Turn the pieces again the following morning.

Snowman Christmas Cake

The snowman runout in this design is brought to 'life' by smaller runout pieces added to complete the picture. The cake is decorated with a double collar and curved side runouts.

Materials

15cm (6 inch) round cake
Apricot glaze
750g (1½lb) almond paste (marzipan)
750g (1½lb/3 cups) royal icing
Selection of food colourings
Clear alcohol (gin or vodka)
15g (½oz) modelling paste

Equipment

25cm (10 inch) round cake board
Waxed paper, board and masking tape
Piping bags
Nos. 00, 0, 1, 2, 3 and 5 piping tubes (tips)
15cm (6 inch) round cake tin or similar curve
Paintbrush and palette
Cake clamp
Foam pieces

Preparation

1 Brush the cake with apricot glaze and cover the top and sides with almond paste. Leave to dry for 4 days.

2 Apply three coats of white royal icing to the top and sides of the cake, allowing each coat to dry before applying the next. Coat the board separately with white royal icing. Leave to dry.

Snowman top piece

3 Trace the snowman design on page 43 (including holly, presents, lantern, scarf, etc.), cover with waxed paper and secure on a smooth, flat board with masking tape.

4 Half-fill a piping bag fitted with a no. 0 or 00 piping tube with white royal icing, and pipe the outlines (see pages 6–7). Flood the various sections of the snowman and the other items with runout consistency royal icing, using the following colours: white, Christmas red, grey (touch of black), Christmas green, dark brown, melon and claret. Leave to dry, and then remove from the waxed paper.

5 Turn the snowman over and flood the back (see page 8). It is not necessary to flood the backs of the other items.

Side snowmen

6 You will need four snowmen for the cake sides. Trace the design on page 43, cover with waxed paper, and place over a curved surface (e.g. a 15cm/6 inch round cake tin or similar curve). Secure with masking tape. Using a no. 0 or 1 piping tube, outline the snowmen with black royal icing (use liquorice black colouring). Flood the various sections of the snowmen with white runout consistency royal icing, taking care not to cover the black outlines. Leave to dry.

masking tape. Pipe all the outlines using a no. 1 piping tube and white royal icing.

11 Flood all of the under collar and the relevant parts of the top collar and board sections with green runout consistency royal icing (use a mixture of mint green and Christmas green food colourings). Flood the remaining areas with white royal icing. Leave to dry. Remove the under collar from the waxed paper.

12 To make the four green lace sections, trace the oval shape from the top collar design four times on to a separate piece of paper. Pipe the outlines on to waxed paper with a no. 0 or 00 piping tube and green royal icing. Pipe a series of straight lines, with dots in between, in the oval shape, and a picot edge (i.e. a series of groups of three dots) around the

7 Paint in the detail on the curved snowmen, using a fine paintbrush and food colours mixed with a little alcohol. The painting can be done with the pieces still in position on the tin, or they can first be removed from the tin and waxed paper.

8 Paint in the detail on the snowman top piece (see page 8), together with the holly, presents, lantern and scarf, etc.

Collars

9 The templates for the top and under collars (see page 44) show one quarter of each collar only. Either trace or photocopy four quarters in order to form complete collars (the photo, right, shows half collars only). The fine dotted line on the top collar template shows the cake line. You will also need four tracings of the board sections

template and an outline of a 7cm (2¾ inch) circle with which to make a plaque.

10 Cover the tracings with waxed paper and secure on a smooth, flat board with

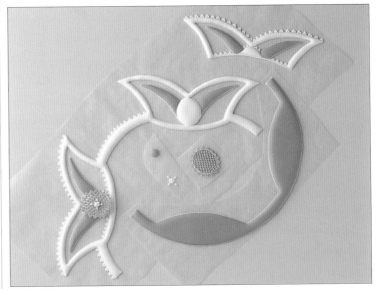

outside. Make a white motif for the middle of each lace section by piping a series of dots together. Leave all the pieces to dry, and then remove from the waxed paper.

◇13◇ Pipe a picot edge around parts of the top collar and board sections using a no. 0 or 00 piping tube and white royal icing. Pipe out four bulbs of green royal icing 6mm (¼ inch) in diameter and leave to dry. Attach the green bulbs to the white ovals on the top collar and sit the green lace sections on top, securing with royal icing. Leave to dry, and then remove from the waxed paper.

Side decoration

◇14◇ Support the cake on its side in a cake clamp. Cut a strip of greaseproof paper the depth and circumference of the cake. Fold into four sections and trace the frame for the linework and the holly design on each section using the side snowman template on page 43. Cut out the inside of the frame from each section, and go over the holly design on the reverse of the paper with a soft pencil. Place the strip of paper around the cake, and secure with masking tape. Lightly trace (see page 9) the holly design on to the sides of the cake.

◇15◇ Pipe 3-2-1 linework in each cut-out section with nos. 3, 2 and 1 piping tubes and white royal icing. Remove the strip of paper and pipe the holly design with a no. 0 piping tube.

When dry, paint the holly green and red. Remove the cake from the cake clamp and place in the centre of the cake board, using royal icing to secure.

Finishing

◇16◇ Attach the runout items to the snowman, using royal icing to secure. Pipe buttons on the snowman. Leave to dry.

◇17◇ Using a no. 1 or 2 piping tube, pipe snow on the round white plaque, leaving an area in the middle clear of 'snow'. Leave to dry. Pipe royal icing on the base of the snowman and stand in an upright position in the smooth area in

the centre of the plaque. Support with foam until dry. Fill in any gaps with more snow. Make snowballs from white modelling paste by rolling small pieces of paste in the palm of your hand. Attach two snowballs behind and two in front of the snowman.

Assembly

◇18◇ Using royal icing to secure, position a curved snowman in the middle of each piped frame on the side of the cake. Pipe a shell border around the base of the cake with a no. 5 piping tube. Immediately place the board sections in position. Pipe snowballs above the shell border and on parts of the board sections, using a no. 2 piping tube.

◇19◇ Still using a no. 2 tube, pipe a line of royal icing around the top edge of the cake, and attach the green under collar. Pipe a picot edge along the inner curves of the under collar where it meets the surface of the cake. Gently place the top collar in position on top of the under collar. Pipe a picot edge around the inside edge of the top collar where it comes into contact with the under collar. This will be enough to secure the top collar. Pipe snowballs just under the collar around the sides of the cake. Place the snowman in the centre of the cake and pipe a picot edge around the plaque. Pipe a snailstrail or shell border around the outside edge of the board with a no. 1 or 2 piping tube and white royal icing.

'Baby' Elephants

This design is suitable for a Christening cake. It is shown here in blue and pink, but peach, lemon, pale green or lilac would also be appropriate.

Materials

125g (4oz/½cup) royal icing
Selection of food colourings
60g (2oz) flower paste
Egg white
Clear alcohol (gin or vodka)
125g (4oz)
sugarpaste
125g (4oz) modelling paste
30g (1oz) pastillage

Equipment

Waxed paper, board and masking tape
Piping bags
Nos. 00, 0, 1 and 3 piping tubes (tips)
Cocktail stick (toothpick)
Paintbrush (size 00) and palette
Patterned rolling pin
15cm (6 inch) round or shaped cake board
Small carnation cutters and blossom cutters
Foam pad and pieces
Small ball modelling tool

Elephants

1 Make a tracing of the 'BABY' elephants design on page 17, cover with waxed paper and secure on a smooth, flat board with masking tape.

2 Half-fill a piping bag with white royal icing and pipe the outlines using a no. 0 piping tube.

3 Flood the various sections with runout consistency royal icing, leaving each one to dry for a few minutes before flooding the next. Use the following colours: blueberry, wedgewood blue, ice blue, peach and grey (touch of black).

4 When dry, remove the runouts from the waxed paper and turn them over. Flood the backs and leave to dry.

5 Turn the runouts back over and over-pipe the trunks with a no. 3 piping tube and grey royal icing (full peak).

Frilling

6 Colour a small piece of flower paste as required, and roll it out until it is very fine. Cut tiny strips and frill the

14

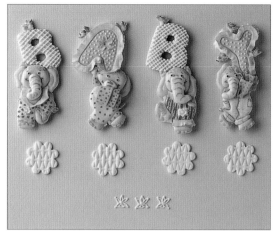

edges with a cocktail stick. Attach frills around the elephants' necks, cuffs and trousers, using egg white to secure them. The sleeves are pleated pieces of paste, gathered at each end.

Painting

7 Paint in the detail on the front and back of the runouts, using a fine brush and food colours mixed with clear alcohol. Carefully paint in the eyes, and the lines on the trunks. Two of the letters are piped with trellis, i.e. criss-cross lines, and the other two are painted. Frills can also be added to some letters. Paint in detail on the birds and leave to dry.

Base

⟨**8**⟩ For the base, colour some sugarpaste and roll it out. Roll over with the patterned rolling pin. Place this on the board and trim. Cut out the half-moon shapes from blue and white modelling paste using templates made from the outlines on page 44. Texture the smallest with the patterned rolling pin.

⟨**9**⟩ Roll out the pastillage, texture with a patterned rolling pin, and cut out four flower shapes with a small carnation cutter, or using the template on page 44. Cut 32 tiny white blossoms (using the smallest blossom cutter) from thinly rolled out flower paste, and cup each one on a foam pad using a small ball tool. Leave everything to dry thoroughly.

⟨**10**⟩ Trace the lace design on page 44 several times, cover with waxed paper, and secure to a smooth, flat board with masking tape. Pipe the design on to the waxed paper using a no. 0 or 00 piping tube and white royal icing. Repeat until you have piped 50 pieces, and leave to dry.

Assembly

⟨**11**⟩ Place the large half-moon shape on the board, then the smaller one on top. Taking one elephant at a time, pipe royal icing on to the undersides of the feet, using a no. 1 piping tube, and stand upright on a pastillage flower shape. Support

with foam until dry. Assemble each elephant in the same way.

⟨**12**⟩ Attach eight blossoms around the feet of each elephant, and pipe a dot of white royal icing in the centre of each blossom. The blossoms give added strength and a neat finish.

⟨**13**⟩ Using royal icing, position each elephant on the half-moon base to spell out the word 'BABY'. Remove the lace pieces from the waxed paper and, using a no. 0 piping tube and white royal icing, attach them around the outside edge of the largest half-moon shape.

Variation

A pink version can be made in exactly the same way. When flooding (step 3 on page 14), use icing coloured with claret, mulberry, grey (touch of black) and melon. Dress the elephants in skirts rather than trousers and add extra frills.

Bride and Groom

This is a traditional-style centrepiece for a wedding cake. The bride and bridegroom are made from runouts, but the bride's veil and train, and the groom's top-hat and parts of their clothing, are made from flower paste and added to give dimension.

Materials

20cm (8 inch) heart-shaped cake
Apricot glaze
1kg (2lb) almond paste
(marzipan)
Clear alcohol (gin or vodka)
1.25kg (2 ½ lb) sugarpaste
Selection of food colourings
125g (4oz/½ cup) royal icing
60g (2oz) flower paste
Egg white
60g (2oz) peach modelling paste
Peach petal dust (blossom tint)
Piping gel (optional)
2.5mm (⅛ inch) wide peach
ribbon to trim cake

Equipment

30cm (12 inch) heart-shaped
cake board
Plastic doily
Waxed paper, board and
masking tape
Piping bags
Nos. 00, 0, 1 and 42 piping tubes
(tips)
Paintbrush and palette
Calyx, small blossom, oval and
frill cutters
Cocktail stick (toothpick)
Foam pad and pieces
Embossers
Scriber
Dog-bone tool

Preparation

 1 Brush the cake with apricot glaze and cover with almond paste. Brush the almond paste with alcohol and cover the cake with sugarpaste which has been coloured with peach paste food colouring. Leave to dry for 2 days.

2 To cover the board, roll out some white sugarpaste, and place a plastic doily over the paste. Roll quite firmly with a rolling pin for a patterned effect. Use to cover the board, trim, and leave to dry for 2 days. Place the cake on the cake board using royal icing to secure.

Bride and groom

3 Trace the bride and groom design on page 45, cover with waxed paper and secure on a smooth, flat board with masking tape.

4 Half-fill a piping bag with white royal icing and pipe the outlines using a no. 0 or 1 piping tube.

5 Flood the various sections with runout consistency royal icing. The bride is mainly white, apart from the face and arms which are flesh coloured (use a touch of paprika). Use peach colouring for the bouquet and chestnut for the hair. The groom has grey trousers, jacket, shoes and cravat (use a touch of black) and a paler shade of grey for the gloves, waistcoat and top-hat. The shirt collar is white. Fill in the hair and face as for the bride.

6 When thoroughly dry, remove the runouts from the waxed paper and turn them over. Flood the backs, making sure they each distinctly show a back view, i.e. the *back* of the bride's veil and dress and the *back* of the groom's head and jacket. Leave to dry.

7 Paint in detail on the bride and groom's faces with a fine paintbrush and food colourings mixed with a little alcohol. Use a touch of dark brown for the eyes and hair, and peach for the mouths.

Clothing

8 Roll out pieces of coloured flower paste thinly, and cut out sections of clothing using templates made from the outlines on page 45 (simple items, such as the collar and turn-ups, can be cut out freehand). For the groom (front view), cut out a white shirt collar and grey lapels, cuffs, turn-ups, cravat and top-hat. Leave to dry. For the back view, cut out grey cuffs, turn-ups and a jacket collar. For the buttonhole, cut out a small blossom shape from

peach-coloured flower paste and frill the edges. Fold the blossom in half and gather up. Attach to the groom's lapel with egg white, and leave to dry.

9 For the bride (front view), cut out a horseshoe shape (see page 45) and paint it silver, with a peach handle. Cut out 22 peach blossoms and prepare as for the groom's buttonhole. Use egg white to attach them to the bouquet and to the garland in the bride's hair. Pipe a pattern on the bodice, sleeves and veil using a no. 0 or 00 piping tube and white royal icing. Leave to dry. For the back view, pipe a pattern on the back of the dress and the veil. Make 14 tiny green leaves and attach them to the sides and back of the bouquet. Leave to dry.

Base

10 Cut out an oval plaque measuring 13 x 8cm (5 x 3¼ inches) from peach modelling paste. (This can be cut out using a template made from the outline on page 45, and can be patterned or plain.) Place a white frill around the outside, using egg white to secure. Leave to dry.

Dust the frill with peach petal dust.

11 Pipe royal icing on the bases of the bride and groom, and stand them upright on the oval plaque, turning them slightly towards each other. Support with foam and leave to dry thoroughly. Pipe shells around the bases of the bride and groom with a no. 42 piping tube and white royal icing.

12 Cut out a veil and train from white flower paste using templates made from the outlines on page 45. Emboss the surface of each piece and frill the edges. Pleat the top edge of the train and attach to the back of the bride's dress with egg white. Gather the top edge of the veil and attach to the top of the bride's head. Allow the pieces to fall naturally and leave to dry.

Cake decoration

13 Mark the top of the cake by lightly scribing the oval flower design from page 45 on to the surface. For the sides, cut a strip of greaseproof (waxed) paper the depth and circumference of the cake. Fold the strip into eight. Trace the extension work template on page 45 on to the folded strip, and cut out. Open the pattern out, place around the cake and hold in position with masking tape. Scribe the top and bottom lines of the pattern on to the sides of the cake. Remove the pattern and trace (see page 9) or scribe the flower design (see page 45) around the cake sides.

Brush embroidery

<14> The brush embroidery on the top and sides of the cake has been piped using a no. 1 piping tube and white, melon, peach and Christmas green royal icing. Piping gel can be added to the royal icing (½ teaspoon gel to 1 tablespoon royal icing) to slow down the drying process. Pipe small sections at a time, starting with the areas furthest away. Using a slightly damp, flat-ended paintbrush,

brush the icing in the direction of the lines on the petals and leaves. When dry, highlight the design by painting or dusting with food colours.

Extension work

<15> Before commencing the extension work, use a no. 0 or 1 piping tube and white royal icing to pipe a snailstrail or small shell border around the base of the cake. Pipe a line just above this and attach a length of 2.5mm (⅛ inch) peach ribbon.

<16> Tilt the cake away from you and, using a no. 1 piping tube and white royal icing, pipe loops around the bottom edge of the cake, following the lower scribed line, not touching the board, to begin the 'bridge'. Pipe a second row of loops on top of the first, making sure the loops touch. Repeat, piping eight rows of loops in total. Leave to dry. Dust the

bridge with peach petal dust and pipe coloured dots at each point.

<17> Tilt the cake towards you and, using the top scribed line on the side of the cake as a guide, pipe straight lines of royal icing from the cake to the bridge, as close together as possible, using a no. 0 or 00 piping tube and peach royal icing. When complete, pipe a further row of white loops along the bridge and dots at each point.

Lace

<18> Trace the lace design on page 45 several times, cover with waxed paper and secure on a smooth, flat board with masking tape. Pipe the design on to the waxed paper using a no. 0 or 00 piping tube. White royal icing has been used for the main part of the lace, with a peach dot piped in the centre. Repeat to make 100 lace pieces. When dry, remove from the waxed paper and attach around the top of the extension work with a no. 0 or 00 piping tube and white royal icing. Pipe peach-coloured dots in between each piece of lace.

<19> For the flowers, cut out large white and small peach calyx shapes from thinly rolled out flower paste. Place the peach shapes on top of the white and cup, securing with egg white. Place a small yellow ball in the centre of each. Attach the flowers to the top of the cake. Place the bride and groom centrepiece on top of the cake, securing with royal icing.

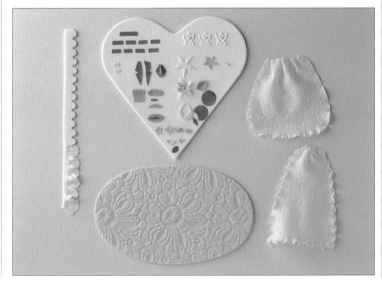

3D Christmas Scene

This design involves flooding on pastillage, a technique I developed for runouts as it is difficult to dry and assemble standing runouts on the same day. Using this method, it is possible to complete a runout project within a few hours.

Materials

125g (4oz) quick-method pastillage (see page 5)
125g (4oz/½ cup) royal icing
Selection of food colourings
Clear alcohol (gin or vodka)
125g (4oz) red sugarpaste

Equipment

Piping bags
Nos. 00, 0 and 1 piping tubes (tips)
Paintbrush and palette
Foam pieces
15cm (6 inch) square cake board
Frill cutter
Robin embosser

Pastillage pieces

1 Roll out the pastillage until it is thin, and cut out the various shapes using templates made from the outlines above and on pages 24 and 46. Dry the pastillage, turning each piece at frequent intervals to avoid distortion of the paste and to ensure even drying.

2 Trace the detail from the templates on to each of the cut-out pieces (see page 9). Pipe the outlines on to the pastillage pieces using a no. 0 piping tube and white royal icing. Some details, such as the baubles on the Christmas tree, are added afterwards.

3 Flood the sections with runout consistency royal icing in appropriate colours. Dry under a lamp, then in a warm, dry place.

Details

4 Pipe in branches on the Christmas tree using a

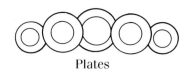

no. 00 piping tube and green royal icing. Pipe the baubles in different coloured icing, or pipe in white icing, and then paint in the colours when dry. Pipe a pattern on the rug and a fringe around the edge.

5 Paint in the remaining detail on all the pieces using a fine paintbrush and food colours mixed with clear alcohol.

Assembly

6 Pipe royal icing on the base of the window piece, and stand at the rear of the floor section. Support in position with pieces of foam until the icing is firm. Secure the plates on top with royal icing. Pipe royal icing on the base of the Christmas tree, and a small bulb of icing on the back at the top. Position against the window on the left-hand side. Secure the rug in place on the floor. Pipe royal icing on the

base of the bear and stand in position on the rug. Attach the watering-can to the bear's hand with royal icing. Place the plant on the right-hand side, and attach the presents to the rug. Finally, position the small bear and the doll at the front of the scene, creating a three-dimensional effect.

7 Cover the square cake board with red sugarpaste and cut the edges with a frill cutter. Emboss the corners with a robin embosser. Position the Christmas scene in the centre.

24

Rocking Horse

This design would be ideal for a birthday cake
and easily adapted for a Christening cake.

Materials

60g (2oz/¼ cup) royal icing
Selection of food colourings
Clear alcohol (gin or vodka)
60g (2oz) flower paste
Egg white
125g (4oz) sugarpaste

Equipment

Waxed paper, board and
masking tape
Piping bags
Nos. 00, 0, 1 and 2 piping
tubes (tips)
Paintbrush and palette
Small round and blossom cutters
Fine scissors
Foam pad and pieces
Small ball modelling tool
20 x 15cm (8 x 6 inch) oval
board
Flower embosser or button
Shell modelling tool
Oval plaque cutter (optional)
Patterned rolling pin (optional)

Rocking horse

1 Trace the rocking horse
illustration on page 26 on
to a piece of tracing paper. Turn
the paper over and make
another tracing of the reversed
design, to give two identical but
opposite sides. Cover the traced
designs with waxed paper and
secure on a smooth, flat board
with masking tape.

2 Half-fill a piping bag with
white royal icing and pipe
the outlines with a no. 0 piping
tube. Flood the various sections
of the rocking horse with runout
consistency royal icing, using
the following colours: claret, violet, blueberry, cream, brown,
peach and white. Leave to dry
thoroughly, and then remove the
runouts from the waxed paper.
(It is not necessary to flood the
backs.) Paint in the facial

features and other details using a fine brush and food colours mixed with alcohol.

Flower paste details

3 Using flower paste in an assortment of colours, e.g. blue, pink, white, yellow and violet, roll tiny sausage shapes for the mane and tail. Attach to both sides of the horse with egg white. Cut out grey circles of thinly rolled out flower paste in three different sizes (using miniature round cutters or piping tubes), and attach to both sides of the body of the rocking horse with egg white.

4 For the tassels, cut out tiny cone-shaped pieces of pink flower paste and make small cuts with fine scissors in the wide end. Roll small balls of paste in a darker shade of pink and attach the two pieces to the sides of the horse, just below the saddle.

5 Cut out blossom shapes in two sizes, medium and small, from peach flower paste. Emboss a pattern on the shapes and attach to the base of the rocking horse with egg white. Cut out two small violet-coloured blossoms, cup on a piece of foam with a small ball tool, and attach to the bear's hat on each piece. Pipe a dot in the centre.

Base

6 Cover the oval board with deep violet sugarpaste and emboss around the edge with a flower embosser or button. Pipe bulbs of white royal icing around the edge with a no. 2 tube.

7 Cut out a white oval plaque measuring 13 x 18cm (5 x 3¼ inches) from sugarpaste, and emboss a pattern around the edge with a shell modelling tool. (This plaque can be cut out using a template made from the outline on this page, and would be suitable patterned or plain.) Leave to dry.

Assembly

8 Pipe white royal icing on the underside of the bases and inside the tops of both sections of the rocking horse, and stand on the white oval plaque. Support with foam if necessary. Attach three small white cupped blossoms either side of the rocking horse where the base meets the board.

Swan Lake

The design of this cake is suitable for an engagement or anniversary, the pair of miniature swans in the centre representing the happy couple. Spaghetti strands have been used to support the reeds and bulrushes.

Materials

20cm (8 inch) octagonal cake
Apricot glaze
1kg (2lb) almond paste
(marzipan)
1.25kg (2½lb) sugarpaste
Selection of food colourings
Clear alcohol (gin or vodka)
125g (4oz/½cup) royal icing
Raw dried spaghetti
60g (2oz) flower paste
Egg white
Pink, moss green and brown
petal dust (blossom tint)
White vegetable fat (shortening)

Equipment

30cm (12 inch) round cake
board
Crimper
Waxed paper, board and
masking tape
Piping bags
Nos. 0, 1 and 42 piping tubes
(tips)
Paintbrush and palette
Calyx cutters and round cutter
Foam pad and pieces
Dog-bone tool
Veining tool

Preparation

1 Brush the cake with apricot glaze and cover with almond paste.

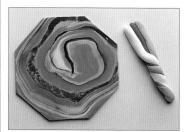

2 Colour small amounts of sugarpaste ice blue and dark blue. Take the pieces of coloured paste and a small amount of white paste, and roll each into a sausage shape using the palm of your hand. Twist the three sausages together, then roll and twist the paste repeatedly to blend the colours and create a marbled effect. Roll out the paste and cut out an octagonal shape using the inset plaque template on page 48.

3 Lay the octagonal template on the centre of the cake and brush the rest of the almond paste with alcohol. Remove the template. Cover the cake with white sugarpaste.

Immediately lay the octagonal template on the cake again, and cut the sugarpaste around it. Remove and discard the octagonal centre piece. Place the marbled plaque in the centre and smooth the edges of the cut section to slant towards the plaque. Leave to dry. Cover the round cake board with marbled sugarpaste and crimp the edges. Leave to dry. Secure the cake on the cake board with royal icing.

Runouts

4 Trace the designs of the swan and swans' wings (above), the reeds, bulrushes, waterlily base and 'CONGRATULATIONS' lettering on page 47, and the side-panel swan on page 31. Cover with waxed paper. Secure on a smooth, flat board with masking tape.

5 Using royal icing, pipe the outlines with a no. 0 tube. You will need two miniature swans and four wings, four side-panel swans, four waterlily bases, two reeds and five bulrushes (two large, three small).

6 Using white runout consistency royal icing,

28

flood the swans, reeds, bulrushes and lettering. Flood the waterlily bases with ice blue royal icing. Leave to dry thoroughly. Pipe a white picot edge, i.e. a series of groups of three white dots, around the curve of each waterlily base.

7 Remove all the runouts from the waxed paper. Turn the miniature swan bodies and the lettering over and flood the backs. It is not necessary to flood the backs of the swans' wings, waterlily bases or side-panel swans.

8 Turn the reeds and bulrushes over and attach 7.5cm (3 inch) strands of spaghetti to the backs with royal icing. Flood the backs of the reeds and bulrushes and part of the spaghetti, leaving about 3.5cm (1 ½ inches) of the stem free. Leave to dry.

9 Paint in detail on the reeds and bulrushes, using brown and green food colourings mixed with alcohol. Paint the stems green. Use green flower paste for the leaves, roll it out thinly, and cut them out freehand with a craft knife (or use templates on page 47). Attach with egg white.

10 Paint in detail on the side-panel swans, using orange and black for the beaks, and blue and white for the bodies.

11 Pipe feathers on the wings of the miniature swans using a no. 0 or 1 piping tube and white royal icing (make sure you have a left and a right wing for each swan). Leave to dry. To assemble a swan, stand the body upright and pipe a small bulb of royal icing on each side. Attach the wings. The swan should then stand up unsupported. Paint orange and black on the beak and black dots for the eyes.

Waterlilies

12 You will need five lilies and ten leaves. Use large, medium, small and miniature calyx cutters and light, medium and dark shades of pink flower paste (use claret or mulberry colouring). For each flower, cut out two large shapes in the palest shade, followed by two medium and two small in the medium shade and two miniature shapes in the darkest pink.

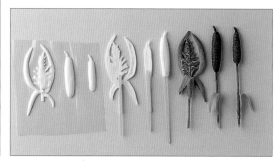

30

Side-panel design

13 Soften the edges of each shape with a dog-bone tool on a piece of foam, and curl the edges in. Take each pair and, using egg white to secure, place one on top of the other so that the petals fall in between. Cup the pairs on foam. Assemble the large, medium, small and miniature petals together, in that order, using egg white.

14 Make a centre from egg yellow and melon-coloured flower paste by rolling out a thin strip 2.5cm (1 inch) long and making tiny cuts all the way along one long side. Roll the strip up, attach in the centre of the flower with egg white, and leave to dry. Dust pink petal dust on the centre petals and moss green on the outside.

15 To make the leaves, cut out 2.5cm (1 inch) rounds from green flower paste (free-hand or using the template on page 47). Soften the edges, and mark lines from the outer edge into the centre with a veining tool. Cut out a 'V', and leave to dry over foam. Dust with brown and green, and brush with vegetable fat.

Pebbles and leaves

16 Cut out leaves as described in step 9 on page 30. To make the pebbles, roll coloured flower paste together, i.e. blue, green, white, brown, etc., break off small pieces and mould into different shapes.

Cake sides

17 Lightly trace or scribe (see page 9) the background for the swans on four alternate sides of the cake. Mark the design for the embroidery in the same way on the remaining four sides, using the design on page 48. Pipe a small shell border around the base of the cake with a no. 42 piping tube and white royal icing. Paint the backgrounds on the four sides with food colours mixed with alcohol. Attach the swans with royal icing.

18 Pipe the embroidery on the other four sides with a no. 0 or 00 piping tube and white and ice blue royal icing. Pipe a line of shells on the cake, the length of the waterlily bases, just below the embroidery, using

a no. 42 piping tube. Attach the bases to the sides of the cake and support with foam until thoroughly dry. Pipe a row of dots on the straight edge where each base comes into contact with the cake, to add strength. Carefully place a waterlily and two leaves on each base and secure with royal icing.

Cake top

19 Pipe small shells with a no. 42 piping tube and white royal icing around the inset plaque. Make small holes in the cake outside the plaque with a sharp instrument and position the reeds and bulrushes in them, securing with royal icing. Attach the two miniature swans on the left of the inset plaque, and a waterlily and two leaves on the right. Position pebbles and leaves around the centre and secure with royal icing. Attach the 'CONGRATULA-TIONS' lettering by piping royal icing on the base of each letter and positioning the pieces on the cake so that the letters slant slightly inwards. Use pieces of foam to support the letters until the icing is thoroughly dry.

Noah's Ark

This very colourful cake would be suitable for a child's birthday. The figures and animals are created for effect and are not to scale.

Materials

30cm (12 inch) round cake
Apricot glaze
1.25kg (2½lb) almond paste (marzipan)
1.25kg (2½lb/5 cups) royal icing
Selection of food colourings
Clear alcohol (gin or vodka)
125g (4oz) modelling paste
Selection of petal dusts (blossom tints)
90g (3oz) pastillage
30g (1oz) flower paste
Egg white

Equipment

36 x 30cm (14 x 12 inch) oval cake board
Waxed paper, board and masking tape
Piping bags
Nos. 0, 1, 2, 22 and 42 piping tubes (tips)
Paintbrush and palette
Veining tool
Patterned rolling pin
Foam pad and pieces
Blossom cutter
Small ball modelling tool

Preparation

1. Cut a pointed oval shape measuring 30 x 23cm (12 x 9 inches) from the 30cm (12 inch) round cake. Brush with apricot glaze and cover the top and sides with almond paste. Leave to dry for 4 days.

2. Apply three coats of white royal icing to the top and sides of the cake, allowing each coat to dry before applying the next. Coat the

enlarge to 105%

board separately with pale green royal icing (use Christmas green colouring). Leave to dry.

Runouts

3 Photocopy the ark and Mr and Mrs Noah illustrations on page 32, enlarging to 105%. Trace the animals on page 34. Cover with waxed paper. Secure on a smooth, flat board with masking tape.

4 Half-fill a piping bag with royal icing and pipe all the outlines using a no. 0 piping tube and white royal icing. Outline two of each animal, but only one giraffe and one elephant, as there is one of each of these in the ark.

5 Flood the various sections with runout consistency royal icing, using a selection of food colourings to colour the royal icing. Try to achieve natural colours for the animals, i.e. cream and autumn leaf for the camels; dark brown and chestnut for the horses, etc.

6 When thoroughly dry, remove the runouts from the waxed paper and turn them over. Flood the backs, noting that the backs of the monkey, lion, penguin, Mr and Mrs Noah and the ark – are different from the fronts. Leave to dry.

7 Paint in detail on all the runouts, using a fine paintbrush and food colourings mixed with alcohol. Pipe a beard on Mr Noah and hair on Mrs Noah, using a no. 1 tube.

Side decorations (optional)

8 The doves and bows on the cake sides can be completed in one of two ways. For the first method, known as 'direct runouts', support the cake on its side in a cake clamp and lightly trace the design (from page 48) on to the cake (see page 9). Outline with royal icing, and fill in with a thicker-than-usual runout consistency royal icing, i.e. made with less water. Dry very rapidly under a heat source, such as an angle-poise lamp.

9 The second method involves tracing the design, covering it with waxed paper, and securing it with masking tape over a curved surface (such as an oval tin). Complete the runouts in the usual way, referring to page 10 for details of curved runouts. When dry, paint in the detail.

10 Decorate the ends of the cake by scribing and piping on the outline on page 36, and filling in with filigree piped using a no. 0 tube and white royal icing.

11 Attach the cake to the board with royal icing, setting it back to within 1cm (½ inch) of the back edge of the cake board. Pipe a ribbon shell border around the top and bottom of the cake using a no. 22 piping tube and pale green royal icing.

Paths, ramp and base

12 Using templates made from the outlines on pages 46–47, cut out two paths from brown modelling paste. Mark a crazy paving effect with a veining tool along the surface of each path. Dust the paving with various shades of brown, cream and skintone petal dust.

13 Cut out the two parts of the ramp from thinly rolled out light brown pastillage. When dry, dust stripes across the pieces, using the colours used for the paths.

14 Cut out a base for the ark (template on page 35) from white pastillage and, when dry, cover with a piece of green modelling paste, textured with a patterned rolling pin. This makes a stronger base.

Trees

15 Trace the design below, cover with waxed paper, and secure on a board with masking tape. Pipe the outlines using a no. 0 piping tube and white royal icing. You will need five trees. Flood the tree trunks with brown runout consistency royal icing, but pipe the top (green) sections of the trees with a thicker consistency royal icing coloured with Christmas green colouring. Leave to dry.

16 Remove the trees from the waxed paper, turn them over and repeat the process on the back. When dry, paint with shades of green and brown.

17 Pipe a row of eight shells in the centre of the ark base using a no. 42 piping tube and pale green royal icing. Stand the ark in an upright position on the base and support with pieces of foam. Leave to dry.

Assembly

18 Position the paths, ramp and ark on the cake and board, and secure with royal icing. Using petal dust, lightly dust blue sky and green grass on the sides of the cake, and dust grass on top of the cake. Attach

the animals by piping a small amount of royal icing on the underside of the feet and standing them in position. Support with foam until thoroughly dry. Attach Mr and Mrs Noah and the tree on the top of the cake in the same way. Pipe royal icing on the base and back of the remaining trees and place in position around the sides of the cake.

19 Cut out numerous blossom shapes in pink, white and yellow flower paste, cup on a piece of foam with a ball tool, secure in position with royal icing and pipe a white dot in the centre of each blossom with a no. 0 piping tube. Make the grass by rolling thin sausages of green flower paste. Fold each piece in half, put two together and attach using egg white.

20 Finally, pipe a small green snailstrail or shell border around the outside edge of the cake board using a no. 2 piping tube and pale green royal icing.

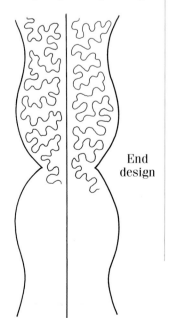

End design

Loving Couple

This design is perfect for the top decoration on an engagement cake, but could also be adapted for an anniversary.

Materials

125g (4oz/½ cup) royal icing
Selection of food colourings
Clear alcohol (gin or vodka)
125g (4oz) modelling paste
125g (4oz) sugarpaste
Egg white

Equipment

Waxed paper, board and masking tape
Piping bags
Nos. 00, 0 and 1 piping tubes (tips)
Paintbrush and palette
Small heart cutter or embosser
15cm (6 inch) round cake board
Foam pieces

Heart

1 Trace the heart design on page 38, cover with waxed paper and secure on a smooth, flat board with masking tape.

2 Half-fill a piping bag with white royal icing, and pipe the outlines on to the waxed paper using a no. 0 or 1 piping tube.

3 Using a no. 00 or 0 piping tube, fill in the middle of the heart with a lacy design made by piping 'S', 'C' and 'X' repeatedly, ensuring all the letters are joined.

4 Flood the outer section of the heart with runout consistency pale lemon royal icing (use melon paste food colouring). When this part of the runout is dry, remove the heart from the waxed paper, turn it over and flood the other side with lemon. Leave to dry thoroughly.

5 Using the illustration on page 38 as a guide, pipe the embroidery design on both sides of the heart using a no. 0 or 00 piping tube and royal icing coloured with blueberry, claret, Christmas green and melon. The variety of colours used for the

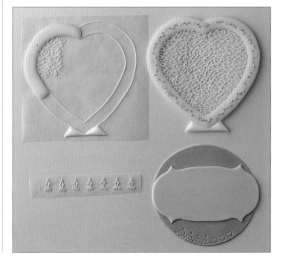

Lace

embroidery creates an effective finish. The same design is also piped on the board edge.

Girl and boy

6 Repeat steps 1 and 2, on page 37, using the girl and boy design above. Colour small amounts of royal icing with the following colours: claret, blueberry, cream, chestnut and Christmas green. Half-fill a small piping bag with runout consistency royal icing in each colour. Flood the various sections, starting with the areas furthest away; use the following flooding order as a guide: log, birds, branches, feet, shoes, trousers, dress, faces, hair, hats, jackets, hands, arms. Flood the rabbit, the four small birds and the two larger birds separately, to be added to the main runout when it is assembled. Leave to dry thoroughly.

7 Remove the runouts from the waxed paper and turn them over. Flood the backs, and leave to dry. Paint in the detail on both sides of the girl and boy runout, and the birds and rabbit, using food colours mixed with clear alcohol.

Base

8 Make a 10cm (3¾ inch) round template and cut out a plaque in blue modelling paste. Emboss the outside edge with a small heart cutter or embosser. Cut out a shaped plaque in pink modelling paste using the outline on this page. Cover the round cake board with pale lemon sugarpaste.

9 Trace the lace design above several times, cover with waxed paper and secure on a smooth, flat board with masking tape. Pipe 50 lace pieces using a no. 0 or 00 tube and pale lemon royal icing.

Assembly

10 Attach the plaques to the lemon-covered board with egg white, starting with the blue, and then placing the pink on top. Pipe some royal icing on the base of the girl and boy runout, and stand upright on the pink plaque. Support it with pieces of foam. Pipe green royal icing at the base for a grass effect, and leave to dry thoroughly.

11 Using royal icing, attach the two larger birds to the top of the heart. Pipe royal icing on to the blue plaque and stand the heart upright, setting it back slightly behind the girl and boy runout. Pipe around the base of the heart and leave to dry. Using royal icing, place the small birds and rabbit in front of the boy and girl runout on the pink plaque. Finally, remove the lace pieces from the waxed paper, and attach them around the blue plaque.

38

Rabbit in a Top-Hat

The design of this runout would suit any special-occasion cake.
The delicate floating plaque adds height to the centrepiece.

Materials

125g (4oz/½ cup) royal icing
Selection of food colourings
Gold petal dust (blossom tint)
Clear alcohol (gin or vodka)
30g (1oz) modelling paste

Equipment

Waxed paper, board and masking tape
Piping bags
Nos. 00, 0, 1 and 2 piping tubes (tips)
Paintbrush and palette
Patterned rolling pin (optional)
Veining tool
Foam pieces
5cm (2 inch) round cutter
Tweezers
15cm (6 inch) round cake board

Runouts

1 Trace the rabbit and plaque designs on page 48, cover with waxed paper, and secure on a smooth, flat board with masking tape. You will need one petal-shaped base plaque and two of the round plaques for 'floating'.

2 Half-fill a piping bag with white royal icing and pipe the outlines on to the waxed paper. Use a no. 0 piping tube for the rabbit, and a no. 1 piping tube for the plaques.

3 Flood the plaques with runout consistency white royal icing. Flood the rabbit and top-hat using the following

colours: claret, blueberry, egg yellow and white. Leave to dry.

Piping and painting

4 Pipe a white picot edge, i.e. a series of groups of three dots, around the outside edge of the petal-shaped plaque. Using a small petal-shaped template made from the linework outline on page 48, and a no. 2 piping tube, pipe white linework on the two round plaques. (Alternatively, these can be left plain.)

5 On the petal plaque, pipe a line with a no. 2 tube about 5mm (¼ inch) in from the edge of the plaque, and following the petal shape all round. Pipe a

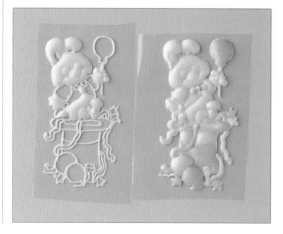

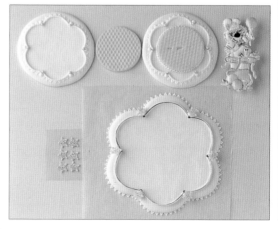

40

second line on top of the first with a no. 1 piping tube and dark blue royal icing (use navy or wedgewood blue). Pipe a third line on top of the second in white with a no. 0 piping tube.

6 ▷ Pipe dots in all the petal indents on all three plaques, and a picot edge on the outside of the linework on the small round plaques. Leave to dry, and then remove the plaques from the waxed paper.

7 ▷ Trace the lace star outline on page 48 six times. Cover with waxed paper, and secure to a board with masking tape. Pipe six pieces of star lace on to the waxed paper with a no. 0 or 00 piping tube and egg yellow royal icing. Fill in with piped filigree. Leave to dry, then dust with gold-coloured petal dust. Remove from the waxed paper and position the stars on top of the piped dots on the petal-shaped plaque. Secure with royal icing.

8 ▷ Remove the rabbit from the waxed paper, turn it over and flood the back, making sure it accurately represents the *back* view of the head and body. When dry, pipe fur on the back of the head and body with white

royal icing and a no. 0 piping tube. Pipe a 'V' pattern on the back of the rabbit's jumper. When thoroughly dry, paint in all the detail with a fine brush and food colours (black, peach and blueberry) mixed with a little alcohol.

Base

9 ▷ Colour the modelling paste with egg yellow and melon. Roll it out and, using the smallest round plaque template, cut out a circle. (This can be left plain or textured with a patterned rolling pin.) Indent the centre with a veining tool to make it easier to stand the rabbit upright when it is assembled. Using royal icing to secure, attach the yellow circle to one of the round white plaques. Pipe a neat pattern of dots around the edge with a no. 0 piping tube and white royal icing. Leave to dry. Pipe royal icing on the underside of the rabbit-and-hat runout and stand it upright on the yellow circle. Support with pieces of foam and leave to dry thoroughly.

Floating plaque

10 ▷ Position the second round white plaque on a 5cm (2

inch) round cutter. Place a piece of foam about 2.5cm (1 inch) in depth on top of the plaque, and sit the first plaque, with the rabbit attached to it, on top. (Note that a plain plaque has been used to illustrate the floating work in the photograph above.)

11 ▷ Using a no. 0 or 00 piping tube and white royal icing, pipe vertical lines from the outer edge of the upper plaque down to the bottom plaque, continuing until you are two-thirds of the way round. Pipe dots in between the lines at the top and bottom to add strength. Leave to dry. Carefully remove the foam with tweezers, then continue piping as before. Finish piping the dots, and leave to dry thoroughly.

Assembly

12 ▷ Secure the floating plaque to the petal-shaped base with royal icing.

13 ▷ Coat the base board with dark blue royal icing, and pipe a zig-zag pattern around the outside edge with yellow royal icing and a no. 00 piping tube. Attach the floating plaque to the board using royal icing to secure.

Templates

Plaque

Snowman top piece

Snowman Christmas Cake
(page 10)

Side snowman
and holly

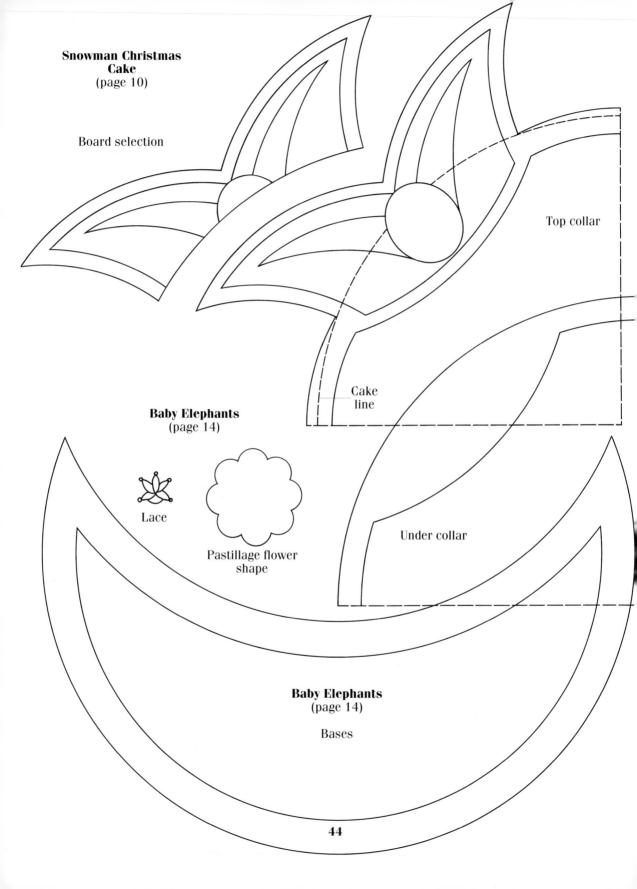

Snowman Christmas Cake
(page 10)

Board selection

Top collar

Cake line

Baby Elephants
(page 14)

Lace

Pastillage flower shape

Under collar

Baby Elephants
(page 14)

Bases

44

Bride and Groom
(page 18)

Train

Horseshoe

Cravat

Top-hat

Lapels

Lace

Veil

Side brush embroidery

Oval plaque

Extension work template

Top brush embroidery

3D Christmas Scene
(page 22)

Noah's Ark
(page 32)
Cake path

Noah's Ark
(page 32)
Board path

Floor

Rug

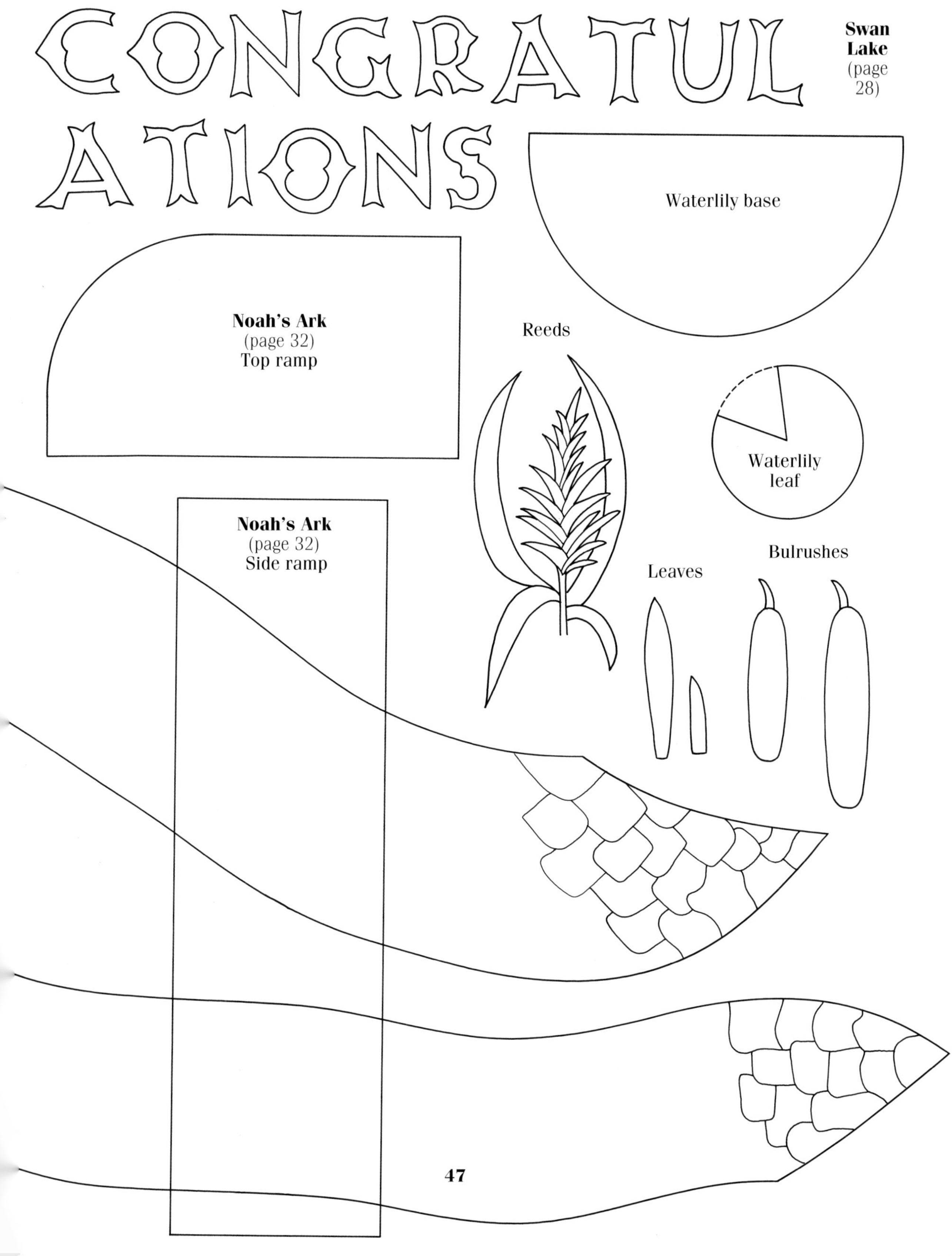

CONGRATUL ATIONS

Swan Lake (page 28)

Waterlily base

Noah's Ark
(page 32)
Top ramp

Reeds

Waterlily leaf

Noah's Ark
(page 32)
Side ramp

Leaves

Bulrushes

47

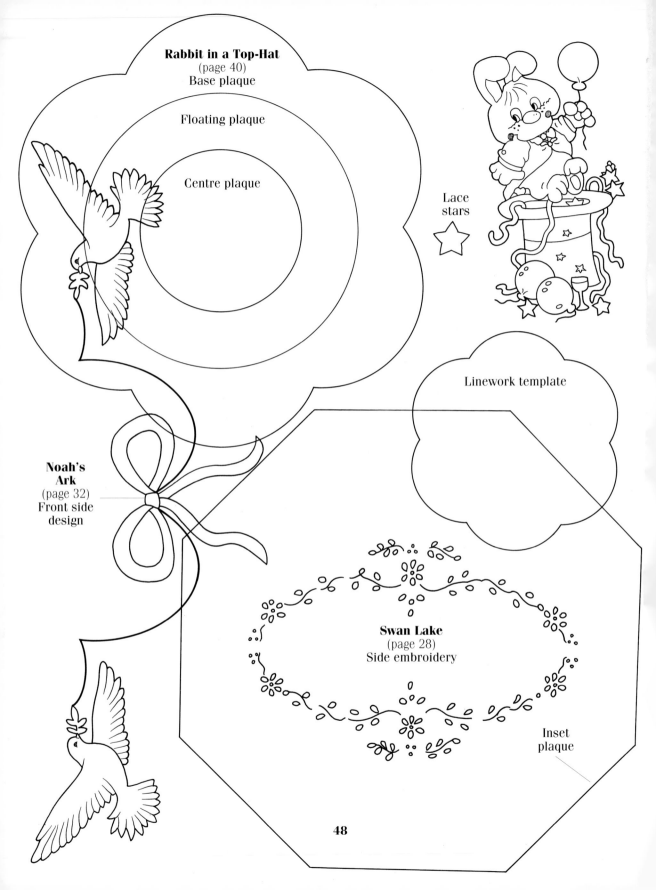

Rabbit in a Top-Hat
(page 40)
Base plaque

Floating plaque

Centre plaque

Lace
stars

Linework template

**Noah's
Ark**
(page 32)
Front side
design

Swan Lake
(page 28)
Side embroidery

Inset
plaque

48